What Columbus Found

It Was Orange, It Was Round

For David and his giant squash . . .
—J. K.

For Dominie, Giliah, and Hillary
—P. B.-F.

ALADDIN PAPERBACKS
An imprint of Simon & Schuster Children's Publishing Division
1230 Avenue of the Americas, New York, NY 10020
Text copyright © 2007 by Jane Kurtz
Illustrations copyright © 2007 by Paige Billin-Frye
Designed by Lisa Vega
The text of this book was set in 24pt Century Oldstyle BT.
Manufactured in the United States of America
First Aladdin Paperbacks edition September 2007
2 4 6 8 10 9 7 5 3 1
Library of Congress Cataloging-in-Publication Data
Kurtz, Jane.
What Columbus found : it was orange, it was round / by Jane Kurtz ;
illustrated by Paige Billin-Frye. — 1st Aladdin Paperbacks ed.
p. cm.
Summary: A rhyming, illustrated story about how Columbus found America—
along with the pumpkins that we grow and bake into pies today.
ISBN-13: 978-0-689-86762-0 (pbk.)   ISBN-10: 0-689-86762-X (pbk.)
ISBN-13: 978-0-689-86763-7 (library binding)   ISBN-10: 0-689-86763-8 (library binding)
1. Columbus, Christopher—Juvenile fiction. [1. Columbus, Christopher—Fiction.
2. Stories in rhyme.] I. Billin-Frye, Paige, ill. II. Title.
PZ8.3.K957Wh 2007
[E] —dc22
2007003740

What Columbus Found

It Was Orange, It Was Round

By Jane Kurtz

ILLUSTRATED BY

Paige Billin-Frye

READY-TO-READ • ALADDIN

New York London Toronto Sydney

Christopher Columbus
was a man on the go.

Was the world round or flat?
Could he find a way to know?

He asked the queen of Spain,
"Will you help?"

No, she would not.

Then she changed her mind.
She gave him money . . .
quite a lot.

He planned to land
in India,
but when he bumped ashore,

he saw the people growing things
he had not seen before.

He took the new things with him
in barrels on his ship.

And then he started home.

It was a lumpy, bumpy trip.

He told the Spanish people
they would soon
see something new.

People waited.
People watched
as a tiny round thing grew.

What did Columbus find?

It had seeds and a rind.
Something fine
on a vine!

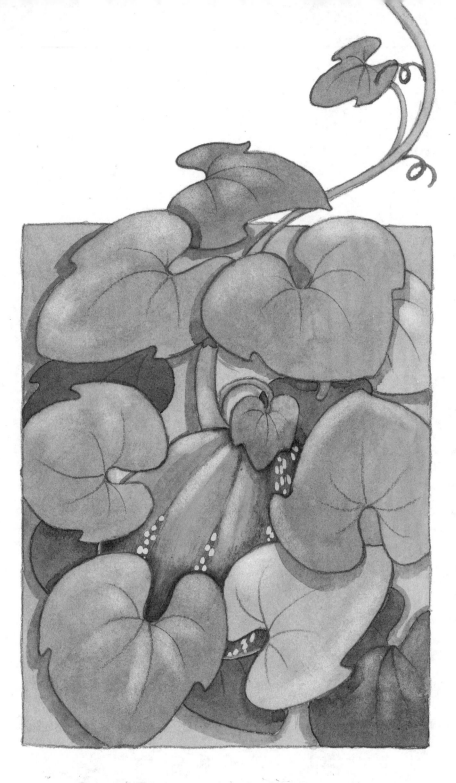

In the garden it kept growing.

It was orange,

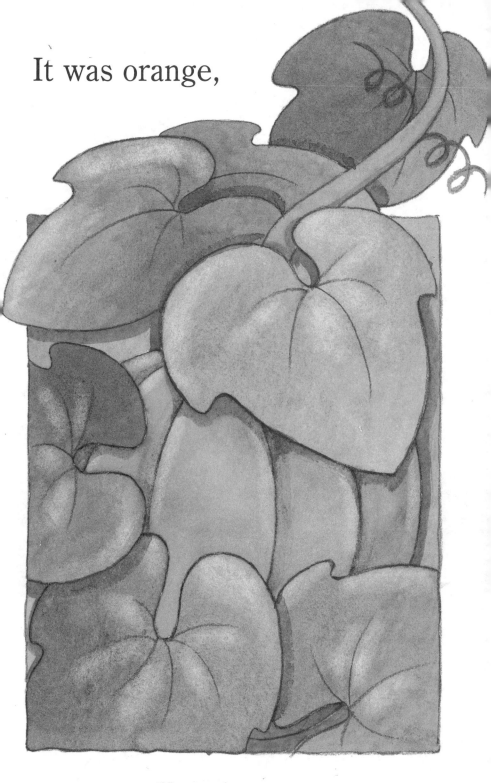

smooth, and big.

Columbus poked and cut it.

And then fed it
to his pig.

But what he found was a gift
that did not go away.

You might eat it in a pie
on this Thanksgiving Day.

Or carve it up.

Or grow it.

And every time you do,

say thank you to America,
the place where
pumpkins grew!